Sixty-Minute Shakespeare

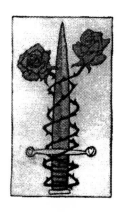

Romeo and Juliet

by Cass Foster

SIXTY-MINUTE SHAKESPEARE

ROMEO AND JULIET

by Cass Foster

♦

from ROMEO AND JULIET
by WILLIAM SHAKESPEARE

© Copyright 2002

published by
Five Star Publications, Inc.
Chandler, Arizona

Sixty-Minute Shakespeare
ROMEO and JULIET

by
Cass Foster

First Edition 1990. Second Edition 1997. Third Edition 1998.
Fourth Edition 2000. Fifth Edition 2001. Sixth Edition 2002.
All rights reserved. Printed in the United States of America.

Library of Congress Cataloging-in-Publication Data

Shakespeare, William, 1564-1616.
Romeo and Juliet (abridged) by Cass Foster—1st Ed.
   p. cm. — (Classics for all ages) (The Sixty-Minute Shakespeare)
Summary: An abridged version of Shakespeare's famous love story,
in which an age-old rivalry between two feuding families leads to a tragic ending.

ISBN: 1-877749-38-9

   1. Married people—Italy—Verona—Juvenile drama. 2. Children's
plays, English. [1. Plays] I. Shakespeare, William. 1564-1616.
Romeo and Juliet. II. Title. III. Series.
PR283.A25 1997
822.3'3—dc21   97-28921
                                                    CIP
                                                    AC

Book Design by Barbara Kordesh
Paul M. Howey, Copy Editor
Sixth Edition edited by Gary E. Anderson

© 1990, 1997, 1998, 2000, 2001 and 2002 by Cass Foster

Five Star Publications, Incorporated
P.O. Box 6698
Chandler, AZ 85246-6698

PHONE: 480.940.8182
FAX: 480.940.8787
WEBSITE: www.fivestarpublications.com/books/60MinuteShakespeare
E-MAIL: shakespeare@fivestarpublications.com

To
Cher Ber
YASDS

Welcome to
THE SIXTY-MINUTE SHAKESPEARE

Thanks to the progressive thinking of so many curriculum developers, Language Arts people and the splendid film work being done by directors such as Kenneth Branagh and Franco Zeffrelli, there has been a phenomenal growth in interest in Shakespeare.

No playwright, past or present, approaches the brilliance and magnitude of William Shakespeare. What other individual has even come close to understanding and then dramatizing the human condition? Just for the fun of it, I am listing (following these introductory remarks) a sample of themes and images so richly developed in the canon of his plays.

Shakespeare's characters are so well-rounded and beautifully constructed that it is common to see them as actual historical figures. When someone mentions Hamlet, Iago, Ophelia, or Puck, we immediately experience images and emotions that come from memories of people we know. We may feel compassion, frustration, sorrow, or pleasure.

As one of the wealthiest people of his times, Shakespeare earned his living as a playwright, theatre manager, actor, and shareholder in the Globe Theatre. He worked tirelessly to entertain. (Theatres presented a new play every day and the average new play had a total of only ten performances over an entire season.) He rebelled against the contemporary theatrical standards (the neo-classical principles that limited dramatic structure throughout France and Italy), he took plots from other published works (making them uniquely his own), and he created a spectacle (without the use of elaborate scenery) to captivate audiences of all social levels.

Imagine the challenge in quieting a crowd of three thousand in a theatre where vendors sell wine, beer, ale, nuts, and cards; where there is no intermission; where birds fly overhead; and where audience members stand near performers. Such was the setting in which Shakespeare's plays were originally staged.

The world's most familiar and successful wordsmith used language to skillfully create images, plot, and a sense of music and rhythm. The purpose behind this series is to reduce (not contemporize) the language. The unabridged Shakespeare simply isn't practical in all situations. Not all educators or directors have the luxury of time to explore the entire text. This is not intended to be a substitute for a thorough study of Shakespeare. It is merely a stepping stone.

I challenge each of you to go beyond the *Sixty-Minute* versions. Use the comfort, appreciation, and self-confidence you will gain to go further. Be proud of the insights and knowledge you acquire but do not be satisfied. The more you read, the more you gain.

May each of you be blessed with an abundance of good health and happiness. I thank you for your interest in our work and hope you are are pleased with what we have done.

May the Verse Be With You!

A COUPLE OF STAGING CONSIDERATIONS

Scenery

There are two excellent reasons theatres rarely use much scenery when staging Shakespeare. The first is related to the number of changes required. If we have to wait every five to ten minutes to watch scenery struck and set up, we end up watching a play about moving lumber. The second is because the audience will lose sight of what the play is about. Audiences need a couple minutes to adjust to the new scenic look of a dazzling waterfall and lush forest. By the time they take it all in and start paying attention to what the actors are saying, it is time to set up the next scene and the audience will be lost.

Location is normally established through dialogue and the use of a few simple props: a throne-like chair for the king's court, a long table with benches for an inn, or a bed for the queen's bed chamber. The key is to keep it simple.

Pacing

You will want to keep things moving all the time. That doesn't mean actors should talk and move quickly; it simply means one scene should flow smoothly to the next without delay or interruption.

As Scene One ends, the actors pick up their props and walk off. Actors for Scene Two enter from a different direction with their props and begin dialogue as soon as they enter the acting area, putting their props in place as they speak. Yes, the audience will still have view of the actors in the first scene, but they will gladly accept this convention if it means taking fifteen minutes off performance time.

TWO HIGHLY RECOMMENDED WEB SITES

www.ShakeSpirit.com

A revolutionary site offering Shakespeare gifts,
Teaching assistance, resources and quotes

www.ShakespeareLRC.com

SHAKESPEARE LEARNING RESOURCE CENTER.
Free Library Dedicated to Shakespeare
and the Performing and Visual Arts.

IMAGES AND THEMES TO LOOK FOR
IN THE VARIOUS PLAYS

Mistaken identity

Wisdom of fools

Insanity

Greed and corruption

Religious persecution

The elements

The supernatural

Darkness and light

Loneliness or isolation

Anti-Semitism

Conspiracy

Revenge

Hypocrisy

Abandonment

Pride

Honor

Violence

Bravery

Rebellion

Savagery

Seduction

Disease or physical decay

Loyalty

War

Marriage

False accusations

Irresponsible power

Destiny or fate

Real or pretended madness

Ambition

Tyranny

Foils or opposites

Spying

Paranoia

Play-acting

Justice

Heavenly retribution

Forgiveness

Witchcraft

Mortality

Self-destruction

Black or white magic

Animals

Nature

Reality vs. illusion

Astrological influence

Characters reforming

Old age

Freedom

Usurping of power

Fertility Suppression

Sexual misadventure

Melancholy

Corrupt society

Love and/or friendship

Multiple meanings of words

Thought vs. action

Impetuous love

Role of women

Human frailty

Preparing for leadership

Charity/Betrayal

THE COMPLETE WORKS
OF WILLIAM SHAKESPEARE

1589 - 1591	Henry VI, Part 1, 2 and 3
1592 - 1593	Richard III
1593 - 1594	Titus Andronicus
1592 - 1594	Comedy of Errors
1593 - 1594	Taming of the Shrew
1594	The Two Gentlemen of Verona
1594 - 1595	Love's Labor's Lost
1594 - 1596	King John
1595	Richard II
1595 - 1596	A Midsummer Night's Dream
1595 - 1596	Romeo and Juliet
1596 - 1597	The Merchant of Venice
1597	The Merry Wives of Windsor
1597 - 1598	Henry IV, Part 1 and 2
1598 - 1599	Much Ado About Nothing
1599	Henry V
1599	Julius Caesar
1599	As You Like It
1600 - 1601	Hamlet
1601 - 1602	Twelfth Night
1601 - 1602	Troilus and Cressida
1602 - 1603	All's Well That Ends Well
1604	Measure for Measure
1604	Othello
1605	The Tragedy of King Lear
1606	Macbeth
1606 - 1607	Antony and Cleopatra
1607 - 1608	Timon of Athens
1607 - 1608	Pericles, Prince of Tyre
1607 - 1608	Coriolanus
1609- 1610	Cymbeline
1609 - 1610	The Winter's Tale
1611	The Tempest
1612 - 1613	Henry VIII
1613	Two Noble Kinsmen (Authorship in question)

23 April 1564 - 23 April 1616

" If we wish to know the force of human genius, we should read Shakespeare. If we wish to see the insignificance of human learning, we may study his commentators."

William Hazlitt (1778-1830) English Essayist. "On the Ignorance of the Learned," in *Edinburgh Magazine* (July 1818).

COMMON QUOTES FROM THE BARD

Romeo and Juliet

> Parting is such sweet sorrow.
> A plague o' both your houses.
> O Romeo, Romeo! Wherefore art thou Romeo?

A Midsummer Night's Dream

> Lord, what fools these mortals be.
> The course of true love never did run smooth.
> To say the truth, reason and love keep little company
>   together now-a-days.

As You Like It

> All that glisters is not gold.
> Love is blind.
> All the world's a stage
>   And all the men and women merely players.
> For ever and a day.

Twelfth Night

> Some are born great, some achieve greatness, and some
>   have greatness thrust upon them.
> Out of the jaws of death.
> O, had I but followed the arts!
> Many a good hanging prevents a bad marriage.

Henry IV, Part 1

> The better part of valor is discretion.
> To give the devil his due.
> He hath eaten me out of house and home.

Henry VI, Part 2

> Let's kill all the lawyers.

The Merry Wives of Windsor

> Better three hours too soon than a minute too late.

Casablanca

> This could be the start of a beautiful friendship.

Macbeth

> Out, damned spot. Out, I say!
> Screw your courage to the sticking place.

Hamlet

> Something is rotten in the state of Denmark.
> To be or not to be. That is the question.
> The lady doth protest too much, methinks.
> Good night, sweet prince, And flights of
>   angels sing thee to thy rest!

The Merchant of Venice

> The devil can cite scriptures for his purpose.

Pericles

> Few love to hear the sins they love to act.

Richard III

> Now is the winter of our discontent.
> Off with his head!
> A horse! A horse! My kingdom for a horse.

Julius Caesar

> Beware the ides of March.
> Friends, Romans, countrymen, lend me your ears.
> It was Greek to me.

Much Ado About Nothing

> The world must be peopled. When I said I would die a
>   bachelor, I did not think I should live till I were married.

Measure for Measure

> The miserable have no other medicine but only hope.

Troilus and Cressida

> To fear the worst oft cures the worse.

The Comedy of Errors

> Unquiet meals make ill digestions.

CAST OF CHARACTERS

Escalus, Prince of Verona
Paris, A young nobleman, kinsman to the Prince
Friar Laurence, A Franciscan
Friar John, A Franciscan
Apothecary
Two Officers of the Prince
Townspeople

Montague, Head of the household
Romeo, Son of Montague
Mercutio, Friend of Romeo, kinsman to the Prince
Benvolio, Friend of Romeo, nephew to Montague *Balthasar,* Servant to Romeo
Abram, Servant to Montague
Lady Montague, Wife of Montague

Capulet, Head of the household
Tybalt, Nephew to Lady Capulet
Gregory, Servant to Capulet
Sampson, Servant to Capulet
Peter, Servant to Juliet's Nurse
Lady Capulet, Wife of Capulet
Juliet, Daughter of Capulet
Nurse, Nanny to Juliet

Locations:
Verona and Mantua

Time:
Fourteenth Century

Prologue

Enter chorus. [Often presented by Friar Laurence.]

Two households, both alike in dignity°,
In fair Verona where we lay our scene,
From ancient grudge break to new mutiny°,
Where civil blood makes civil hands unclean.
From forth the fatal loins of these two foes
A pair of star-crossed° lovers take their life;
Whose misadventured piteous overthrows
Doth with their death bury their parents' strife.
The fearful passage of their death-marked° love,
And the continuance of their parents' rage,
Which, but their children's end, naught could remove,
Is now the two hours' traffik° of our stage;
The which if you will with patient ears attend,
What here shall miss, our° toil shall strive to mend.

ACT I, SCENE 1.
THE MARKET PLACE.

Enter Sampson and Gregory of the House of Capulet.

Greg. Draw thy tool! Here comes two of the house of
Montagues.

Samp. My naked weapon is out. Quarrel! I will back thee.

Enter Abram and Balthasar.

Dignity: social position.   *Mutiny:* discord.   *Star-crossed:* ill-fated.
Death-marked: doomed to die.   *Traffik:* business.   *Our:* i.e., the actors.

Greg. I will frown as I pass by, and let them take it as they list.

Samp. Nay, as they dare. I will bite my thumb at them; which is disgrace to them, if they bear it.

Abr. Do you bite your thumb at us, sir?

Samp. I do bite my thumb, sir.

Abr. Do you bite your thumb at us, sir?

Samp. [Aside to Gregory.] Is the law on our side if I say aye?

Greg. [Aside to Sampson.] No.

Samp. No, sir, I do not bite my thumb at you, sir; but I bite my thumb, sir.

Greg. Do you quarrel, sir?

Abr. Quarrel, sir? No, sir.

Greg. You lie.

Samp. Draw, if you be men. Gregory, remember thy swash-ing° blow.

They fight.

Benvolio enters and beats down their rapiers.

List: please.   *Swashing:* crashing.

Benvolio. Part, fools!
  Put up your swords. You know not what you do.

Enter Tybalt.

Tybalt. What, art thou drawn among these heartless hinds°?
  Turn thee, Benvolio. Look upon thy death.

Ben. I do but keep the peace. Put up thy sword,
  Or manage it to part these men with me.

Tybalt. What, drawn, and talk of peace? I hate the word as I
  hate hell, all Montagues, and thee. Have at thee, coward!

They all fight.

*Enter Old Capulet and his wife on one side and Old
Montague and his wife on the other, followed by townspeople.*

Cap. What noise is this? Give me my long sword, ho!

Mon. Thou villain Capulet! Hold me not, let me go.

Enter Prince Escalus and his guards.

Prince. Rebellious subjects, enemies to peace,
  On pain of torture, from these bloody hands
  Throw your mistempered° weapons to the ground
  And hear the sentence of your moved° Prince.

Heartless hinds: timid servants.   *Mistempered:* i.e., made for an evil purpose.
Moved: angry.

3

All carefully set their weapons down.

Prince. Three civil brawls bred of an airy word,
   By thee, Old Capulet, and Montague,
   Have thrice disturbed the quiet of the streets.
   If ever you disturb our streets again,
   Your lives shall pay the forfeit° of the peace.
   For this time all the rest depart away.
   You, Capulet, shall go along with me;
   And Montague, come you this afternoon,
   To know our farther pleasure in this case.
   Once more, on pain of death, all men depart.

ACT I, SCENE 2.
STREET NEAR THE CAPULET HOUSE.

Enter Capulet, County Paris, and Capulet's servant.

Paris. But now, my lord, what say you to my suit?

Cap. But saying o'er what I have said before:
   My child is yet a stranger in the world,
   She hath not seen the change of fourteen years;
   Let two more summers wither in their pride
   Ere we may think her ripe to be a bride.

Paris. Younger than she are happy mothers made.

Cap. And too soon marred are those so early made.
   The earth hath swallowed all my hopes but she.
   Woo her, gentle Paris, get her heart;
   My will to her consent is but a part.

Forfeit: punishment.

4

Cap. [To the servant, giving him a paper.] Go, sirrah, trudge
     about
  Through fair Verona, find those persons out
  Whose names are written there, and to them say,
  My house and welcome on their pleasure stay.

Exit Capulet and Paris.

Servant. Find them out whose names are written here! I can
     never find what names the writing person hath writ here.
     I must to the learned.

Enter Benvolio and Romeo, laughing.

Romeo. Ah, god-den°, good fellow.

Servant. G-d° gi' god-den. I pray, sir, can you read?

Romeo. Ay, if I know the letters and the language.

Servant is about to depart.

[Romeo] Stay fellow. I can read.

Servant hands Romeo the list and Romeo reads.

  "Signoir Martino and his wife and daughters; Count
  Anselmo and his beauteous sister; the lady widow of
  Vitruvio, Signoir Placentio and his lovely nieces; mine
  Uncle Capulet, his wife and daughters; my fair niece
  Rosaline; Signoir Valentio and his cousin Tybalt."

---

god-den: good evening

5

[Romeo, returning the list.] A fair assembly. Wither should
   they come?

Servant. Up.

Romeo. Whither?

Servant. To supper, to our house.

Romeo. Whose house?

Servant. My master's.

Romeo. Indeed, I should have asked you that before.

Servant. Now I'll tell you without asking. My master is the
   great rich Capulet; and if you be not of the house of
   Montagues, I pray come and crush° a cup of wine. Rest
   you merry! *[He exits.]*

Ben. At this same ancient feast° of Capulet's
   Sups the fair Rosaline whom thou so lov'st,
   With all the admired beauties of Verona.
   Go thither, and with unattainted eye°
   Compare her face with some that I shall show,
   And I will make thee think thy swan a crow.

Romeo. I'll go along, no such sight to be shown,
   But to rejoice in splendor of mine own. *[They exit.]*

Crush: drink.   *Ancient feast:* regular family gathering   *Unattainted eye:* open
mind.

ACT I, SCENE 3.
CAPULET'S HOUSE.

Enter Lady Capulet, Juliet, and Nurse.

Juliet. What is your will?

Lady C. Nurse, give us leave awhile,
   We must talk in secret.—Nurse, come back again.
   I have remembered me, thou'st hear our counsel.
   Thou knowest my daughter's of a pretty age.

Nurse. Faith, I can tell her age unto an hour.

Lady C. She's not fourteen.

Nurse.   I'll lay fourteen of my teeth—
   And yet, to my teen be it spoken, I have but four—
   Come Lammas° Eve at night shall she be fourteen.
   Susan and she (G-d rest all Christian souls!)
   Were of an age. Well, Susan is with G-d;
   She was too good for me. But, as I said,
   on Lammas Eve at night shall she be fourteen.

Lady C. Enough of this. I pray thee hold thy peace.

Nurse. Peace, I have done. G-d mark thee to His grace!
   Thou wast the prettiest babe that e'er I nursed.
   An I might live to see thee married once, I have my wish.

Lammas Eve: a holy feast was held on Lammastide, August 1.

Lady C. Marry, that "marry" is the very theme
   I came to talk of. Tell me, daughter Juliet,
   How stands your disposition° to be married?

Juliet. It is an honor that I dream not of.

Lady C. Well, think of marriage now. Younger than you,
   Here in Verona, ladies of esteem,
   Are made already mothers. By my count,
   I was your mother much upon these years
   That you are now a maid. Thus then in brief:
   The valiant Paris seeks you for his love.

Nurse. A man, young lady! Lady, such a man
   As all the world—why he's a man of wax°.

Lady C. What say you? Can you love the gentleman°?
   This night you shall behold him at our feast.
   Read o'er the volume of young Paris' face,
   And find delight writ there with beauty's pen;
   So shall you share all that he doth possess,
   By having him, making yourself no less.

Nurse. No less? Nay, bigger! Women grow by men!

Lady C. Speak briefly, can you like of Paris' love?

Juliet. I'll look to like, if looking liking move°. *[They exit.]*

Disposition: inclination.   *Man of war:* i.e., molded into perfection.   *Can you...the gentleman:* it was common practice at this time for parents to arrange their children's marriage.   *I'll look...liking move:* i.e.. I'll be open-minded.

ACT I, SCENE 4.
STREET NEAR THE CAPULET HOUSE.

*Enter Romeo, Mercutio, Benvolio with five or six other
maskers and torch bearers.*

Romeo. Give me a torch. I am not for this ambling;
   Being but heavy°, I will bear the light.

Mer. Nay, gentle Romeo. We must have you dance.

Romeo. Not I, believe me. You have dancing shoes
   With nimble soles; I have a soul of lead
   So stakes me to the ground I cannot move.

Mer. You are a lover. Borrow Cupid's wings
   And soar with them above a common bound°.
   Come, we burn daylight, ho!

Romeo. We mean well in going to the masque°;
   But 'tis no wit° to go.

Mer.   Why, may one ask?

Romeo. I dreamt a dream tonight°.

Mer.   And so did I.

Romeo. Well, what was yours?

Heavy: sad.   *Bound:* leap. [Many dances of the day had leaping steps.]   *Masque:*
masquerade party.   *Wit:* wise.   *Tonight:* last night.

9

Mer.   That dreamers often lie.

Romeo. In bed asleep, while they do dream things true.

Mer. O, then I see Queen Mab° hath been with you.
   She is the fairies' midwife°, and she comes
   In shape no bigger than an agate stone°
   On the forefinger of an alderman,
   Drawn with a team of little atomies°
   Athwart men's noses as they lie asleep;
   Her wagon spokes made of long spinners' legs,
   The cover, of the wings of grasshoppers;
   Her traces, of the smallest spider's web;
   Her collars, of the moonshine's wat'ry beams;
   Her whip, of cricket's bone; the lash, of film;
   Her wagoner, a small grey-coated gnat,
   Not half so big as a round little worm
   Pricked from the lazy finger of a maid,
   Her chariot is an empty hazelnut. This is that very Mab
   That plaits the manes of horses in the night
   And bakes the elflocks° in foul sluttish hairs,
   Which once untangled much misfortune bodes.
   This is the hag°, when maids lie on their backs,
   That presses them and learns them first to bear,
   Making them women of good carriage°.
   That is she—

Romeo. Peace, peace, Mercutio, peace.
   Thou talk'st of nothing.

Queen Mab: queen of the fairies.   *Fairies' midwife:* i.e., gives birth to men's fan-
tasies.   *Agate stone:* stone set in a ring   *Atomies:* tiny creatures.   *Elflocks:* matted
hair from lack of brushing or grooming   *Hag:* evil spirit.   *Of good carriage:* able
to bear children.

10

Mer.   True, I talk of dreams;
   Which are the children of an idle brain,
   Begot of nothing but vain° fantasy;
   Which is as thin of substance as the air,
   And more inconstant than the wind.

Ben. This wind you talk of blows us from ourselves.
   Supper is done, and we shall come too late.

Romeo. I fear too early; for my mind misgives
   Some consequence°, yet hanging in the stars,
   Shall bitterly begin his fearful date
   With this night's revels and expire the term
   Of a despised life, closed in my breast,
   By some vile forfeit of untimely death.
   But he that hath the steerage° of my course
   Direct my sail! On, lusty gentlemen!

Ben. Strike, drum.

They march off.

Vain: worthless.   *Consequence:* event to come.   *Steerage:* direction.
Please note:
*Not everyone realizes it is not only illegal to photocopy copyrighted material but by
photocopying (and reducing sales) small publishing houses like ours will not be able to
generate sufficient resources to create additional works. We appreciate your understanding and assistance.*

ACT I, SCENE 5.
CAPULET HOUSE.

Servingmen quickly set the scene as musicians move into place. Enter Capulet, Lady Capulet, Juliet, Tybalt, Paris, Nurse, maskers, and Gentlewomen to the maskers.

Capulet. Welcome, gentlemen! Ladies that have their toes
  Unplagued with corns will walk a bout° with you.
  Ah, my mistress, which of you all
  Will now deny to dance? She that makes dainty,
  She I'll swear hath corns. Come, musicians, play.

Music plays and they dance. Juliet dances with Paris.

Romeo. [To a servant.] What lady's that which doth enrich
  the hand of yonder knight?

Servant. I know not, sir.

Romeo. O, she doth teach the torches to burn bright!
  It seems she hangs upon the cheek of night
  Like a rich jewel in an Ethiop's ear—
  Beauty too rich for use, for earth too dear!
  So shows a snowy dove trooping with crows
  As yonder lady o'er her fellows shows.
  Did my heart love till now? Forswear it, sight!
  For I never saw true beauty till this night.

Walk a bout: dance a turn.

12

Tybalt. This, by his voice, should be a Montague.
  Fetch me my rapier, boy.

Servant exits.

Tybalt. Now by the stock and honor of my kin,
  To strike him dead I hold it not a sin.

Cap. Why, how now kinsman. Wherefore storm you so?

Tybalt. Uncle, this is a Montague, our foe;
  A villain that has hither come in spite
  To scorn at our solemnity° this night.

Cap. Young Romeo is it?

Tybalt.   'Tis he, that villain Romeo.

Cap. Content thee, gentle cuz, let him alone.
  'A bears him° like a portly° gentleman,
  And, to say truth, Verona brags of him
  To be a virtuous and well-governed youth.
  I would not for the wealth of this town
  Here in my house do him disparagement.
  Therefore be patient, take no note of him.

Tybalt. It fits when such a villain is a guest.
  I'll not endure him.

Cap.   He shall be endured.
  Am I the master here, or you? Go to!

Solemnity: festivity.   'A bears him: he conducted himself   Portly: well-mannered.

13

Tybalt. I will withdraw; but this intrusion shall,
   Now seeming sweet, convert to bitter gall. *[He exits.]*

Romeo. If I profane with my unworthiest hand
   This holy shrine, the gentle fine is this:
   My lips, two blushing pilgrims, ready stand
   To smooth that rough touch with a tender kiss.

Juliet. Good pilgrim, you do wrong your hand too much,
   Which mannerly devotion shows in this:
   For saints have hands that pilgrim's hands do touch,
   And palm to palm is holy palmers'° kiss.

Romeo. Have not saints lips, and holy palmers too?

Juliet. Aye, pilgrim, lips that they must use in prayer.

Romeo. O, then, dear saint, let lips do what hands do!
   They pray; grant thou, lest faith turn to despair.
   Thus from my lips, by thine my sin is purged.
   [Kisses her.]

Juliet. Then have my lips the sin that they have took.

Romeo. Sin from my lips? O trespass sweetly urged!
   Give me my sin again. *[Kisses her.]*

Nurse. Madam, your mother craves a word with you.

Romeo. What is her mother?

Palmer: pilgrim to religious shrines.

Nurse.   Marry, bachelor,
  Her mother is the lady of the house.
  I tell you, he that can lay hold of her
  Shall have the chinks °.

Romeo.   Is she a Capulet?
  O dear° account. My life is my foe's debt.

Ben. Away, be gone, the sport is at the best°.

Benvolio and Romeo start to leave.

Juliet. [To the Nurse.] What's he that follows there?

Nurse. I know not.

Juliet. Go ask his name. *[Nurse crosses to Romeo.]*
  If he be married my grave is like to be my wedding bed.

Nurse. His name is Romeo, and a Montague;
  The only son of your great enemy.

Juliet. My only love sprung from my only hate!
  Too early seen unknown, and known too late!
  Prodigious° birth of love it is to me
  That I must love a loathed enemy.

They exit.

Have the chinks: share her great wealth.   *Dear:* costly.   *The sport... best:* i.e., let's leave while we are ahead.   *Prodigious:* ominous.

ACT II, SCENE 1.
STREET NEAR THE CAPULETS.

Enter Romeo alone.

Romeo. Can I go forward when my heart is here?
   Turn back, dull earth°, and find thy center° out.

He climbs behind a wall.

Enter Benvolio and Mercutio.

Ben. Romeo! My cousin Romeo! Romeo!

Mer.   He is wise,
   And, by my life, hath stol'n him home to bed.

Ben. He ran this way, and leapt this orchard wall.
   Call, good Mercutio.

Mer.   Nay, I'll conjure° too.
   Romeo! Humors! Madman! Passion! Lover!
   Appear thou in the likeness of a sigh;
   Speak but one rhyme, and I am satisfied!
   I conjure thee by Rosaline's right eyes,
   By her high forehead and her scarlet lip,
   By her fine foot, straight leg, and quivering thigh,
   And the demesnes° that there adjacent lie,
   That in thy likeness thou appear to us!

Earth: body.   *Center:* head.   *Conjure:* call him up by magic.   *Demesnes:* private
regions.

Ben. An if he hear thee, thou wilt anger him.

Mer. This cannot anger him. My invocation
Is fair and honest°: in his mistress' name,
I conjure only but to raise up him.

Ben. Come, he hath hid himself among these trees
To be consorted with the humorous night.
Blind is his love, and best befits the dark.

Mer. If love be blind, love cannot hit the mark°.
Romeo, good night. I'll to my tuckle-bed°;
This field-bed is too cold for me to sleep.
Come, shall we go?

Fair and honest: proper.   *Mark:* target.   *Tuckle-bed:* bed on casters.

ACT II, SCENE 2.
CAPULET'S ORCHARD.

Juliet is above at her window. Enter Romeo below.

Romeo. But soft! What light through yonder window
  breaks? It is the East, and Juliet is the sun!
  Arise, fair sun, and kill the envious moon,
  Who is already sick and pale with grief
  That thou her maid art far more fair than she.
  It is my lady; O, it is my love!
  O that she knew she were!
  She speaks, yet she says nothing. What of that?
  See how she leans her cheek upon her hand!
  O that I were a glove upon that hand,
  That I might touch that cheek!

Juliet.   Aye me!

Romeo.   She speaks.

Juliet. O Romeo, Romeo! Wherefore° art thou Romeo?
  Deny thy father and refuse thy name!
  Or, if thou wilt not, be but sworn my love,
  And I'll no longer be a Capulet.

Romeo. [Aside.] Shall I hear more, or shall I speak at this?

Juliet. 'Tis by thy name that is my enemy.
  Thou art thyself, though not a Montague.
  What's Montague? It is not hand nor foot,

Wherefore: why.

20

[Juliet] Nor arm, nor face, nor any other part
　　Belonging to a man. O, be some other name!
　　What's in a name? That which we call a rose
　　By any other name would smell as sweet.
　　So Romeo would, were he not Romeo called.
　　　　　　　　　　　　Romeo, doff thy name;
　　And for that name, which is no part of thee,
　　Take all myself.

Romeo.　　　　　　　　　　I take thee at thy word.
　　Henceforth I never will be Romeo.

Juliet. What man art thou that, thus bescreened in night,
　　So stumblest on my counsel?

Romeo.　　　　　　　　　　By a name
　　I know not how to tell thee who I am.
　　My name, dear saint, is hateful to myself,
　　Because it is an enemy to thee.

Juliet. My ears have yet not drunk a hundred words
　　Of that tongue's utterance, yet I know the sound.
　　Art thou not Romeo, and a Montague?

Romeo. [Climbs to her window.] Neither, fair maid, if either
　　thee dislike.

Juliet. How camest thou hither, tell me, and wherefore?

Romeo. With love's light wings did I o'erperch these walls;
　　For stony limits cannot hold love out
　　Therefore thy kinsmen are no let to me.

Juliet. If they do see thee, they will murder thee.

Romeo. I have night's cloak to hide me from their sight;
   And but thou love me, let them find me here.
   My life were better ended by their hate
   Then death prorogued°, wanting of thy love.

Juliet.   O gentle Romeo,
   If thou dost love, pronounce it faithfully.
   Or if thou thinkest I am too quickly won,
   I'll frown and be perverse, and say thee nay.

Romeo. Lady, by yonder blessed moon I swear,
   That tips with silver all these fruit-tree tops—

Juliet. O, swear not by the moon, the inconstant moon,
   That monthly changes in her circled orb,
   Lest that thy live prove likewise variable.

Romeo. What shall I swear by?

Juliet.   Do not swear at all;
   Or if thou wilt, swear by thy gracious self,
   Which is the god of my idolatry, and I'll believe thee.

Romeo.   If my heart's dear love—

Juliet. Well, do not swear. Although I joy in thee,
   I have no joy of this contract tonight.

Prorogued: prolonged.

22

Romeo. O, wilt thou leave me so unsatisfied?

Juliet. What satisfaction canst thou have tonight?

Romeo. The exchange of thy love's faithful vow for mine.

Juliet. I hear some noise within. Dear love, adieu!

Nurse calls from offstage.

[Juliet] Anon°, good nurse! Sweet Montague, be true.
  Stay but a little, I will come again.

Juliet exits.

Romeo. O blessed, blessed night! I am afeard,
  Being in night, all this is but a dream,
  Too flattering-sweet to be substantial.

Juliet enters.

Juliet. Three words, dear Romeo, and good night indeed.
  If that thy bent of love be honorable,
  Thy purpose marriage, send me word tomorrow,
  By one that I'll procure° to come to thee,
  Where and what time thou wilt perform the rite;
  And all my fortunes at thy foot I'll lay
  And follow thee, my lord, throughout the world.

Anon: coming.   *Procure:* arrange.

23

Nurse. [Offstage.] Madam!

Juliet. I come, anon°—But if thou meanst not well,
   I do beseech thee—

Nurse. [Offstage.] Madam!

Juliet.   By-and-by I come—
   To cease thy suit and leave me to my grief.
   Tomorrow will I send.

Romeo.   So thrives my soul—

Juliet. A thousand times good night!

She exits.

Romeo. A thousand times the worse, to want thy light!
   [Climbing down.] Love goes toward love as schoolboys
   from their books;
   But love from love, toward school with heavy looks.

Juliet. [Returns to her window.] Hist! Romeo, hist! Romeo!

Romeo. [Climbs back up.] My sweet?

Juliet. What o'clock tomorrow shall I send for thee?

Romeo. By the hour of nine.

Juliet. I will not fail. 'Tis twenty years till then…
   I have forgot why I did call thee back.

Anon: soon.

Romeo. Let me stand here till thou remember it.

Juliet. I shall forget to have thee still stand there,
  Rememb'ring how I love thy company.

Romeo. And I'll stay to have thee still forget. . .

Juliet. 'Tis almost morning. I would have thee gone—
  And yet no farther than a wanton's° bird,
  That lets it hop a little from her hand.

Romeo. I would I were that bird.

Juliet.   Sweet, so would I.
  Yet I should kill thee with much cherishing.
  Good night, good night. Parting is such sweet sorrow,
  That I shall say good night till it be morrow.

She exits.

Romeo. Sleep dwell upon thine eyes, peace in thy breast!
  Would I were sleep and peace, so sweet to rest!
  Hence will I to my ghostly° father's cell,
  His help to crave and my dear hap° to tell.

He climbs down and exits.

Wanton: heedless.   *Ghostly:* spiritual.   *Dear hap:* good fortune.

ACT II, SCENE 3.
FRIAR LAURENCE'S CELL.

Enter Friar Laurence with a basket.

Friar. The grey-eyed morn smiles on the frowning night,
  Chequ'ring the eastern clouds with streaks of light;
  From forth day's path and Titan's fiery wheels°.
  Now, ere the sun advance his burning eye
  The day to cheer and night's dank° dew to dry,
  I must up-fill this osier cage° of ours
  With baleful weeds and precious-juiced flowers.

Enter Romeo.

Romeo. Good morrow, father.

Friar.   Benedicite°!
  What early tongue so sweet saluteth me?
  Our Romeo hath not been in bed tonight.
  G-d pardon sin! Wast thou with Rosaline?

Romeo. With Rosaline, my ghostly father? No.
  I have forgot that name, and that name's woe.

Friar. That's my good son! But where hast thou been then?

Romeo. I'll tell thee ere thou ask it me again.
  I have been feasting with mine enemy,
  Where on a sudden one hath wounded me
  That's by me wounded. Both our remedies
  Within thy help and holy physic° lies.

Titan's fiery wheels: the sun god's chariot wheels.   *Dank:* wet.   *Osier cage:* wicker
basket.   *Benedicite:* G-d bless you.   *Physic:* medicine.

26

Friar. Be plain, good son, and homely in thy drift°.
  Riddling confession finds but riddling shrift°.

Romeo. Then plainly know my heart's dear love is set
  On the fair daughter of rich Capulet;
  As mine on hers, so hers set on mine,
  And all combined°, save what thou must combine
  By holy marriage. When, and where, and how
  I'll tell thee as we pass°; but this I pray,
  That thou consent to marry us today.

Friar. Holy Saint Francis! What a change is here!
  Is Rosaline, that thou didst love so dear,
  So soon forsaken? Young men's love then lies
  Not truly in their hearts, but in their eyes.

Romeo. I pray thee, chide° me not. Her I love now
  Doth grace for grace and love for love allow. The other
  did not so.

Friar. In one respect I'll be;
  For this alliance may so happy prove
  To turn your household's rancor to pure love.

Romeo. O, let us hence. I stand on sudden haste.

Friar. Wisely, and slow. They stumble that run fast.

They exit.

Homely in thy drift: get to the point.   *Shrift:* absolution.   *Combined:* agreed.
Pass: move along.   *Chide:* scold.

ACT II, SCENE 4.
STREET IN VERONA

Enter Benvolio and Mercutio.

Mer. Where the devil should this Romeo be?
　　Came he not home tonight?

Ben. Not to his father's. I spoke with his man.

Mer. Why that same pale hard-hearted wench, that
　　Rosaline, torments him so that he will sure run mad.

Ben. Tybalt, the kinsman of old Capulet,
　　Hath sent a letter to his father's house.

Mer. A challenge, on my life.

Ben. Romeo will answer it.

Mer. Any man that can write may answer a letter.

Ben. Here comes Romeo, here comes Romeo.

Mer. Signior Romeo, bon jour! There's a French salutation
　　to your French slop. You gave us the counterfeit° fairly
　　last night.

Romeo. Good morrow to you both. What counterfeit did I
　　give you?

Counterfeit: fake coin.

Mer. The slip°, sir, the slip. Can you not conceive?

Enter the Nurse, followed by her man, Peter, holding up the train of her dress.

Romeo. Here's goodly gear°.

Mer. A sail, a sail°.

Nurse. Peter!

Peter. Anon.

Nurse. My fan, Peter.

Mer. Good Peter, to hide her face; for her fan's the fairer of the two.

Nurse. Gentlemen, can any of you tell me where I may find the young Romeo?

Romeo. I can tell you but young Romeo will be older when you have found him than he was when you sought him. I am the youngest of that name, for a fault of a worse.

Nurse. If you be he, sir, I desire some confidence with you.

Mercutio moves behind the Nurse and lifts her dress over his head.

Slip: counterfeit coin.   *Here's goodly gear:* this ought to be fun.   *A sail, a sail:* the call of sailors when they see a ship on the horizon.

Mer. A bawd°, a bawd, a bawd. So ho°!

Romeo. What hast thou found?

Mer. No hare...Romeo, will you come to your father's?
   Will to dinner thither.

Romeo. I will follow.

Mer. Farewell, ancient lady, farewell *[Sings]* "lady, lady, lady."

Mercutio and Benvolio exit laughing.

Nurse. Marry, farewell! I pray you, sir, what saucy merchant
   was this that was so full of his ropery°?

Romeo. A gentleman, nurse, that loves to hear himself talk.

Nurse. Now, afore G-d, I am so vexed that every part about
   me quivers. Scurvy° knave! Pray you, sir, a word; and as
   I told you, my young lady bid me inquire you out.

Romeo.   Bid her devise
   Some means to come to shrift° this afternoon;
   And there she shall at Friar Laurence's cell
   Be shrived and married. *[Hands her a gold coin.]* Here is
   for thy pains.

Bawd: procuress.   *So ho:* the cry of a hunter upon sighting game.   *His ropery:*
criminal behavior.   *Scurvy:* contemptuous.   *Shrift:* confession.   *Shrived:*
absolved from sin.

Nurse. No, truly, sir; not a penny.

She takes the coin from him before he can return it to his purse.

Nurse. This afternoon, sir? Well, she shall be there.

Romeo. Farewell. Commend me to thy lady.

Nurse. Aye, a thousand times.

Exit Romeo.

[Nurse] Peter!

Peter. Anon.

Nurse. Peter, take my fan, and go before, and apace°.

We hear the sound of twelve chimes on a clock as they exit.

Apace: quickly.

ACT II, SCENE 5.
CAPULET'S ORCHARD.

Enter Juliet.

Juliet. The clock struck nine when I did send the nurse;
In half an hour she promised to return.
Perchance she cannot meet him. That's not so.
O she is lame!

Enter Nurse and Peter.

[Juliet] O G-d, she comes! O honey nurse, what news?
Hast thou me with him? Send thy man away.

Nurse. Peter, stay at the gate.

Exit Peter.

Juliet. Now, good sweet nurse why lookst thou sad?
Though news be sad, yet tell them merrily.

Nurse. I am weary, give me leave awhile°. *[Nurse sits.]*
Fie, how my bones ache!
What a jaunce° have I had!

Juliet. I wouldst thou had my bones, and I thy news.
Nay, come, I pray thee speak. Good, good nurse, speak.

Nurse. Jesu, what haste! Can you not stay awhile?
Do you not see that I am out of breath?

Give…awhile: leave me alone.   *Jaunce:* difficult journey.

Juliet. How art thou out of breath when thou hast breath
   To say to me that thou art out of breath?
   Is thy news good or bad, answer to that.
   What says he to our marriage? What of that?

Nurse. Lord, how my head aches! What a head have I!
   [Juliet massages the Nurse's head.] My back. *[Juliet rubs
   her back.]* O, to the other side! *[Juliet does so.]*
   Beshrew° your heart for sending me about
   To catch my death with jauncing up and down.

Juliet. In faith, I am sorry that thou art not well.
   Sweet, sweet, sweet nurse, tell me, what says my love?

Nurse. Your love says, like an honest gentleman, and a
   courteous, and a kind, and a handsome, and, I warrant, a
   virtuous—Where is your mother?

Juliet. Where is my mother? Why she is within.
   Where should she be? How oddly thou repliest!
   "Your love says, like an honest gentleman,
   'Where is your mother?'"

Nurse. Have you got leave to go to shrift today?

Juliet. I have.

Nurse. Then hie° you hence to Friar Laurence' cell;
   There stays a husband to make you a wife.

Juliet. Hie to high fortune. Honest nurse, farewell!

Beshrew: curse [though used casually].   *Hie:* hurry.

ACT II, SCENE 6.
FRIAR LAURENCE'S CELL.

Enter Friar Laurence and Romeo.

Friar. So smile the heavens upon this holy act
   That after-hours with sorrow chide us not!

Romeo. Amen, amen! But come what sorrow can,
   It cannot countervail° the exchange of joy
   That one short minute gives me in her sight.
   It is enough I may call her mine.

Friar. These violent delights have violent ends
   And in their triumph die, like fire and powder,
   Which, as they kiss, consume.

Enter Juliet.

[Friar] Here comes the lady. O, so light a foot
   Will ne'er wear out the everlasting flint.

Juliet. Good even to my ghostly° confessor.

Romeo. Let rich music's tongue
   Unfold the imagined happiness that both
   Receive in either by this dear encounter.

Friar. Come, come with me, and we will make short work;
   For, by your leaves, you shall not stay alone
   Till Holy Church incorporate two in one. *[They exit.]*

Countervail: equal.   *Ghostly:* spiritual.

ACT III, SCENE 1.
A PUBLIC PLACE.

Enter Mercutio, Benvolio, and men.

Ben. I pray thee, good Mercutio, let's retire.
  The day is hot, the Capels° are abroad,
  And if we meet, we shall not 'scape a brawl,
  For now these hot days, is the mad blood stirring.

Mer. Thy head is as full of quarrels as an egg is full of meat;
  thou hast quarreled with a man for coughing in the
  street, because he hath wakened thy dog that hath lain
  asleep in the sun. And yet thou wilt tutor me from
  quarreling?

Enter Tybalt and men.

Ben. By my head, here come the Capulets.

Mer. By my heel, I care not.

Tybalt. Gentlemen, good den. A word with one of you.

Mer. And but one word with one of us?
  Couple it with something; make it a word and a blow

Tybalt. You shall find me apt enough to that, sir, and you
  will give me occasion.

Mer. Could you not take some occasion without giving?

Capels: Capulets.   *Good-den:* good evening or good afternoon.

37

Tybalt. Mercutio, thou consortest° with Romeo.

Mer. Consort°? What, dost thou make us minstrels?
   Here's my fiddlestick; here's that shall make you dance.

Ben. We talk here in the public haunt of men.
   Either withdraw unto some private place,
   And reason coldly° of thy grievances,
   Or else depart. Here all eyes gaze on thee.

Mer. Men's eyes were made to look, and let them gaze.
   I will not budge for no man's pleasure, I.

Romeo enters.

Tybalt. Then peace be with you. Here comes my man.
   Romeo, the love I bear thee can afford
   No better term than this: thou art a villain.

Romeo. Tybalt, the reason that I have to love thee
   Doth much excuse the appertaining rage
   To such greeting. Villain am I none.
   Therefore farewell. I see thou knowest me not.

Tybalt. Boy, this shall not excuse the injuries
   That thou hast done me; therefore turn and draw.

Romeo. I do protest I never injured thee,
   But love thee better than thou canst devise°

Consortest: associates.   *Consort:* musician [a group of musicians were known as
consorts].   *Coldly:* calmly.   *Devise:* imagine.

[Romeo] Till thou shalt know the reason of my love;
And so, good Capulet, which name I tender°
As dearly as mine own, be satisfied.

Mer. O calm, dishonorable, vile submission! *[Draws his
rapier.]* Tybalt, you ratcatcher°, will you walk°?

Tybalt. What wouldst thou have with me?

Mer. Good king of cats, nothing but one of your nine lives.

Tybalt. I am for you. *[Draws his rapier.]*

Romeo. Gentle Mercutio, put thy rapier up.

Mer. Come sir, your *passado*°!

They fight.

Romeo. Tybalt, Mercutio, the Prince expressly hath
Forbid this bandying in Verona streets.

Fight continues. Eventually Romeo pulls Mercutio aside.

[Romeo] Hold Tybalt! Good Mercutio!

*Romeo and Mercutio have their backs to Tybalt. Tybalt
thrusts his blade into Mercutio. Tybalt and his men quickly
flee. Romeo and his friends assume Mercutio is clowning
around.*

Tender: cherish.   *Ratcatcher:* i.e., cat.   *Will you walk:* invitation to a duel.
Passado: step forward then thrust weapon.

39

Mer.   I am hurt.
    A plague o' both your houses! I am sped.
    Is he gone and hath nothing?

Ben.   What, art thou hurt?

Mer. Aye, aye, a scratch, a scratch. Marry, 'tis enough.
    Where is my page? Go, villain, fetch a surgeon. *[Page
    exits.]*

Romeo. Courage, man. The hurt cannot be much.

Mer. No, 'tis not so deep as a well, nor so wide as a church
    door; but 'tis enough, 'twill serve. Ask for me tomorrow,
    and you shall find me a grave man. A plague o' both your
    houses! Why the devil came you between us! I was hurt
    under your arm.

Romeo. I thought all for the best.

Mer. Help me into some house, Benvolio,
    Or I shall faint. A plague o' both your houses!
    They have made worms' meat of me. I have it,
    And soundly too—your houses!

Benvolio helps Mercutio off.

Romeo. This gentleman, the Prince's near ally°
    My very° friend, hath got his mortal hurt
    In my behalf. O sweet Juliet,
    Thy beauty hath made me effeminate°
    And in my temper softened valor's steel.

Ally: kinsman.   *Very:* loyal.   *Effeminate:* soft, unwilling to fight.

Romeo picks up Mercutio's rapier as Benvolio enters.

Ben. O Romeo, Romeo, brave Mercutio's dead!

Romeo. This day's black fate on moe° days doth depend,
   This but begins the woe others must end.

Tybalt and his friends return.

Ben. Here comes the furious Tybalt back again.

Romeo. Alive in triumph, and Mercutio slain?
   Away to heaven, respective lenity°,
   And fire-eyed fury be my conduct° now! Tybalt,
   Mercutio's soul is but a little way above our heads,
   Staying for thine to keep him company.
   Either thou or I, or both, must go with him.

Tybalt. Thou wretched boy, that didst consort him here,
   Shalt with him hence.

Romeo.   This° shall determine that.

They fight and eventually Tybalt is slain.

Ben. Romeo, away, be gone!
   Stand not amazed°. The Prince will doom thee death
   If thou art taken. Hence, be gone, away.

Romeo. O, I am fortune's fool°! *[Romeo exits.]*

Moe: more.   *Lenity:* mercy.   *Conduct:* guide.   *This:* i.e., my rapier.   *Amazed:*
speechless.   *Fool:* plaything.

41

Enter Montagues, Capulets, Prince, and Prince's train.

Prince. Where are the vile beginners of this fray?

Ben. O noble Prince, I can discover° all
    The unlucky manage° of this fatal brawl.
    There lies the man, slain by young Romeo,
    That slew thy kinsman, brave Mercutio.

Lady Cap. Tybalt, my cousin! O my brother's child!

Prince. Benvolio, who began this bloody fray?

Ben. Tybalt, here slain, whom Romeo's hand did slay.
    Tybalt hit the life
    Of stout° Mercutio, and then Tybalt fled,
    But by-and-by comes back to Romeo,
    Who had but newly entertained revenge,
    And to't they go like lightning; for, ere I
    Could draw to part them, was stout Tybalt slain;
    And, as he fell, did Romeo turn and fly.
    This is the truth, or let Benvolio die.

Lady Cap. He is a kinsman to the Montague;
    Affection makes him false, he speaks not true.
    I beg for justice, which thou, Prince, must give.
    Romeo slew Tybalt; Romeo must not live.

Montague. He was Mercutio's friend;
    His faults concludes but what the law should end,
    The life of Tybalt.

Discover: explain.   *Manage:* events.   *Stout:* valiant.

Prince.   And for that offense
Immediately we do exile him hence.
Let Romeo hence in haste,
Else, when he is found, that hour is his last.
Bear hence this body and attend our will.

Gregory and Sampson carry off Tybalt's body as all exit.

ACT III, SCENE 2.
CAPULET'S ORCHARD.

Enter Juliet.

Juliet. Gallop apace, you fiery-footed steeds°,
   Towards Phoebus' lodging! Such a wagoner
   As Phaeton° would whip you to the west
   And bring in cloudy night immediately.
   Come, night; come, Romeo; come, thou day in night
   For thou wilt lie upon the wings of night
   Whither that new snow upon a raven's back.
   Come, gentle night; come, loving, black-browed night.

Nurse enters.

[Juliet] Now, nurse, what news? Why dost thou wring thy
   hands?

Nurse. Ah, well-a-day°! He's dead, he's dead, he's dead!
   Whoever thought it? Romeo!

Juliet. What devil art thou that dost torment me thus?

Steeds: horses of the sun god, Phoebus.   *Phaeton:* son of Phoebus, killed by Zeus
for recklessly driving the sun chariot.   *Well-a-day:* alas.

43

Nurse. O Tybalt, Tybalt, the best friend I had!
   That ever I should live to see thee dead!

Juliet. What storm is this that blows so contrary?
   Is Romeo slaughtered, and is Tybalt dead?
   My dear-loved cousin, and my dearer lord?

Nurse. Tybalt is gone and Romeo banished;
   Romeo that killed him, he is banished.

Juliet. O G-d! Did Romeo's hand shed Tybalt's blood?

Nurse. It did, it did! Alas the day, it did!

Juliet. O serpent's heart, hid with a flowering° face!
   Did ever dragon keep° so fair a cave?
   Beautiful tyrant! Fiend angelical!
   Just opposite to what thou justly seem'st
   A damned saint, an honourable villain!

Nurse. Give me some aqua vitae°.
   These griefs, these woes, these sorrows make me old.
   Shame to Romeo.

Juliet.   Blistered be thy tongue
   For such a wish! He was not born to shame.
   Upon his brow shame is ashamed to sit;
   O, what a beast was I to chide at him!

Nurse. Will you speak well of him that killed your cousin?

Flowering: youthful.   *Keep:* protect.   *Aqua vitae:* brandy.

Juliet. Shall I speak ill of him that is my husband?
  Ah, poor my lord, what tongue shall smooth thy name°
  When I, thy three-hours' wife, have mangled it?
  But wherefore, villain, didst thou kill my cousin?
  That villain cousin would have killed my husband.
  Back, foolish tears, back to your native spring!
  I'll to my wedding bed;
  And death, not Romeo, take my maidenhead!

Nurse. Hie to your chamber. I'll find Romeo
  To comfort you. I wot° well where he is.
  Hark ye, your Romeo will be here tonight.
  I'll to him; he is hid at Laurence' cell.

Juliet. O, find him! Give this ring to my true knight
  And bid him come to take his last farewell.

They exit.

Smooth thy name: speak well of you.   *Wot:* know.

ACT III, SCENE 3.
FRIAR LAURENCE IS FOUND IN HIS CELL.

Friar. Come, come forth; come forth thou fearful man.
   Affliction is enamored of thy parts,
   And thou art wedded to calamity.

Romeo enters.

Romeo. Father, what news? What is the Prince's doom?

Friar. Not body's death, but body's banishment.

Romeo. Ha, banishment. Be merciful, say "death;"
   For exile hath more terror in his look,
   Much more than death. Do not say "banishment."

Friar. Hence from Verona art thou banished.
   Be patient, for the world is broad and wide.

Romeo. [Falling to the ground.] There is no world without°
   Verona walls, but purgatory, torture, hell itself.

Friar. O deadly sin! O rude unthankfulness!
   Thy fault our law calls death; but the kind Prince,
   Taking thy part, hath rushed aside the law,
   And turned that black word death to banishment.
   This is dear mercy, and thou seest it not.

Romeo. 'Tis torture, and not mercy. Heaven is here,
   Where Juliet lives.

Without: beyond.

46

Sound of knocking from offstage.

Friar. Arise; one knocks. Good Romeo, hide thyself.

More knocking.

[Friar] Hark, how they knock! Who's there? Romeo arise;
Thou wilt be taken.—Stay awhile.—Stand up!
Who knocks so hard? What's your will?

Nurse. [Offstage.] Let me come in, and you shall know my
errand. I come from Lady Juliet.

Friar.   Welcome, then.

Enter Nurse.

Nurse. O holy Friar, O, tell me, holy Friar, Where is my
lady's lord, where's Romeo?

Friar. There on the ground, with his own tears made
drunk.

Nurse. Stand up, stand up! Stand, and you be a man.
For Juliet's sake, for her sake, rise and stand!

Romeo. Nurse, spakest thou of Juliet? How is it with her?
Does she think me an old murderer,
Now I have stained the childhood of our joy
With blood removed but little from her own?

Nurse. O, she says nothing sir, but weeps and weeps;
   And now falls on her bed, and then starts up,
   And Tybalt calls; and then on Romeo cries,
   And then down falls again.

Romeo. O, tell me, Friar, tell me,
   In what vile part of this anatomy
   Doth my name lodge? Tell me that I may sack
   The hateful mansion. *[He draws his dagger.]*

Friar.   Hold thy desperate hand.
   Art thou a man? Thy form cries out thou art;
   Thy tears are womanish, thy wild acts denote
   The unreasonable fury of a beast.
   Go get thee to thy love, as was decreed,
   Ascend her chamber, hence and comfort her.
   But look thou stay not till the watch be set°,
   For then thou canst not pass to Mantua,
   Where thou shalt live till we can find a time
   To blaze° your marriage, reconcile your friends°,
   Beg pardon of the Prince, and call thee back.

Romeo returns his dagger to its sheath.

Nurse. O Lord, I could have stayed here all the night
   To hear good counsel. O, what learning is!
   My lord, I'll tell my lady you will come.
   Here sir, a ring she bid me give you, sir.
   Hie you, make haste, for it grows very late. *[She exits.]*

Romeo. How well my comfort° is revived by this.

Friar. Go hence. Good night. *[They exit.]*

Watch be set: guard be posted.   *Blaze:* announce.   *Your friends:* both your families.   *Comfort:* happiness.

ACT III, SCENE 4.
THE CAPULET HOUSE.

Enter Capulet, Lady Capulet and Paris.

Cap. Things have fallen out°, sir, so unluckily
  That we have had no time to move our daughter°.

Paris. These times of woe afford no time to woo.
  Madam, good night. Commend me to your daughter.

Lady Cap. I will, and know her mind early tomorrow;
  Tonight she's mewed up to her heaviness.

Cap. Sir Paris, I will make a desperate tender
  Of my child's love. I think she will be ruled
  In all respects by me; nay more, I doubt not.
  Wife, go you to her ere you go to bed;
  Acquaint her here of my son Paris' love
  And bid her (mark you me?) on Wednesday next—
  But, soft! What day is this?

Paris.   Monday, my lord.

Cap. Well, Wednesday is too soon.
  A Thursday let it be—a Thursday tell her,
  She shall be married to this noble earl.

Paris. My lord, I would that Thursday were tomorrow.

Cap. Well, get you gone. A Thursday be it then. *[They exit.]*

Fallen out: happened.   *Move out daughter:* influence Juliet on your behalf.

49

ACT III, SCENE 5.
ROMEO AND JULIET ARE IN JULIET'S BED
OR AT HER WINDOW.

Juliet. Wilt thou be gone? It is not yet near day.
   It was the nightingale, and not the lark,
   That pierced the fearful hollow of mine ear.

Romeo. It was the lark, the herald of the morn.
   I must be gone and live, or stay and die.

Juliet. Yond light is not daylight; I know it, I.
   It is some meteor that the sun exhales
   To be to thee this night a torchbearer
   And light thee on thy way to Mantua.
   Therefore stay yet; thou needst not to be gone.

Romeo. Let me be ta'en, let me be put to death.
   I am content, so thou wilt have it so.

Sound of a lark.

Juliet. It is, it is! Hie hence, be gone, away!
   It is the lark that sings so out of tune,
   Straining harsh discords and unpleasing sharps°.
   Some say the lark makes sweet division;
   This doth not so, for she divideth us.
   O, now be gone! More light and light it grows.

Romeo. More light and light—more dark and dark our
   woes!

Nurse enters hastily.

Unpleasing sharps: shrill notes.

50

Nurse. Madam!

Juliet. Nurse?

Nurse. Your lady mother is coming to your chamber.
     The day is broke. Be wary, look about. *[Nurse exits.]*

Juliet. Then, window, let day in, and let life out.

Romeo. Farewell, farewell! One kiss and I'll descend.

They kiss and he climbs down.

Juliet. O thinkst thou we shall ever meet again?

Romeo. I doubt it not; and all these woes shall serve
     For sweet discourses in our time to come. *[He exits.]*

Juliet. O G-d, I have an ill-divining soul°!

Lady Capulet enters.

Lady Cap. Why, how now Juliet?

Juliet.   Madam, I am not well.

Lady Cap. Evermore weeping for your cousin's death?
     But now I'll tell thee joyful tidings, girl.

Juliet. And joy comes well in such a needy time.
     What are they, I beseech your ladyship?

An ill-divining soul: premonition of evil.

51

Lady Cap. Marry, my child, early next Thursday morn
   The gallant, young, and noble gentleman,
   The County° Paris, at Saint Peter's Church,
   Shall happily make thee there a joyful bride!

Juliet. Now by Saint Peter's Church, and Peter too,
   He shall not make me there a joyful bride!

Capulet enters.

Cap. How now? A conduit°, girl? What, still in tears?
   How now wife? Have you delivered to her our decree?

Lady Cap. Ay, sir; but she will none°.

Cap. How? She will none? Doth she not give us thanks?
   Is she not proud? Doth she not count her blest,
   Unworthy as she is, that we have wrought
   So worthy a gentleman to be her bridegroom?

Juliet. Not proud you have, but thankful that you have.

Cap. How, how! How, how! Choplogic°? What is this?
   "Proud"—and "I thank you"—and "I thank you not"—
   Go with Paris to Saint Peter's Church,
   Or I will drag thee on a hurdle° hither.
   Out, you green-sickness carrion°! Out, you baggage!

Lady Cap. Fie, fie! What, are you mad?

Juliet. Good father, I beseech you on my knees.

County: count or earl.   *Conduit:* water fountain.   *None:* have nothing to do
with it.   *Choplogic:* idle chatter.   *Hurdle:* device to drag criminals to their execu-
tion.   *Green-sickness carrion:* pale piece of flesh.

[Juliet] Hear me with patience but to speak a word.

Cap. Hang thee, young baggage! Disobedient wretch!
   I tell thee what—Get thee to church on Thursday
   Or never after look me in the face. *[Nurse enters.]*
   Speak not, reply not, do not answer me!
   If you be not, hang, beg, starve, die in the streets,
   For, by my soul, I'll never acknowledge thee,
   Nor what is mine shall never do thee good. *[He exits.]*

Juliet. Is there no pity sitting in the clouds
   That sees into the bosom of my grief?
   O sweet my mother, cast me not away!

Lady Cap. Talk not to me, for I'll not speak a word.
   Do as thou wilt, for I have done with thee. *[She exits.]*

Juliet. O G-d! O Nurse, how shall this be prevented?

Nurse. I think it best you married with the County.
   O, he's a lovely gentleman!
   Romeo's dishclout to° him.
   Beshrew my very heart,
   I think you are happy in the second match,
   For it excels your first.

Juliet. Well, thou hast comforted me marvelous much.
   Go in and tell my lady I am gone,
   Having pleased my father, to Laurence' cell,
   To make confession and to be absolved. *[Nurse exits.]*
   I'll to the Friar to know his remedy.
   If all else fail, myself have power to die. *[Juliet exits.]*

Dishclout to him: dirty dishwater compared to him.

53

ACT IV, SCENE 1.
FRIAR LAURENCE' CELL

Enter Friar Laurence and Juliet.

Juliet. Come weep with me—past hope, past cure, past help!

Friar. O Juliet, I already know thy grief;
   It strains° me past the compass° of my wits.
   I hear thou must, and nothing may prorogue° it,
   On Thursday next be married to this County.

Juliet. Tell me not, Friar, that thou hear hearst of this,
   Unless you tell me how I may prevent it.

Friar. Hold, daughter. I do spy a kind of hope.
   If thou darest, I'll give thee remedy.

Juliet. I will do it without fear or doubt,
   To live an unstained wife to my sweet love.

Friar. Hold then. Go home, be merry, give consent
   To marry Paris. Wednesday is tomorrow.
   Tomorrow night look that thou lie alone;
   Let not the nurse lie with thee in thy chamber.
   Take thou this vial, being then in bed,
   And this distilling° liquor drink thou off;
   When presently through all thy veins shall run
   A cold and drowsy humor°, for no pulse
   Shall keep his native progress, but surcease°;

Strains: taxes.   *Compass:* limits.   *Prorogue:* postpone.   *Distilling:* powerful
Humor: fluid.   *Native:* natural.   Surcease: stop.

[Friar] No warmth, no breath, shall testify thou livest;
   The rose in thy lips and cheeks shall fade
   To paly ashes, thy eyes' windows° fall
   Like death when he shuts up the day of life.
   Thou shalt continue two-and-forty hours,
   And then awake as from a pleasant sleep.
   In the meantime, against thou shalt awake,
   Shall Romeo by my letters know our drift°;
   And hither shall he come; and he and I
   Will watch thy waking, and that very night
   Shall Romeo bear thee hence to Mantua.

Juliet. Give me, give me!

She takes the vial.

Friar. Hold! Get you gone, be strong and prosperous °
   In this resolve. I'll send a Friar with speed
   To Mantua, with my letters to thy lord.

Juliet. Love give me strength! And strength shall help
   afford°. Farewell, dear father.

They exit.

Windows: lids.   *Drift:* plan.   *Prosperous:* successful.   Afford: succeed.

57

ACT IV SCENE 2.
CAPULET'S HOUSE.

Enter Capulet, Lady Capulet, Nurse, and one servant.

Cap. What, is my daughter gone to Friar Laurence?

Nurse. Aye, forsooth.

Cap. Well, he may chance to do some good on her.

Enter Juliet.

[Cap] How now, my headstrong? Where have you been
   gadding?

Juliet. Where I have learnt me to repent the sin
   Of disobedient opposition
   To you and your behests°, and am enjoined
   By holy Laurence to fall prostrate here
   To beg your pardon. Pardon, I beseech you!

Cap. Send for the County. Go tell him of this. *[Servant
   exits.]*

Juliet. Nurse, will you go with me into my closet
   To help me sort such needful ornaments
   As you think fit to furnish me tomorrow?

Cap. Go, Nurse, go with her. We'll to church tomorrow.

Exit Juliet and Nurse.

Cap.   I will walk myself
   To County Paris, to prepare him up
   Against tomorrow°. My heart is wondrous light.

Behests: commands.   *To prepare...tomorrow:* to help him get ready in time.

ACT IV, SCENE 3.
JULIET'S CHAMBER.

Enter Juliet and the Nurse.

Juliet. Aye, those attires are best; but, gentle nurse,
   I pray thee leave me to myself tonight.

Enter Lady Capulet.

Lady Cap. What, are you busy, ho? Need you my help?

Juliet. No madam, we have culled such necessaries
   As are behooveful° for our state tomorrow.
   So please you, let me now be left alone,
   And let the nurse this night sit up with you;
   For I am sure you have your hands full all
   In this so sudden business.

Lady Cap.   Good night.
   Get thee to bed and rest, for thou hast need.

Exit Lady Capulet and the Nurse.

Juliet. Farewell! G-d knows when we shall meet again.
   I have a faint cold fear thrills° through my veins
   That almost freezes up the heat of life.
   Come, vial.
   What if this mixture do not work at all?

Behooveful: needed.   *Thrills:* pierces.

59

[Juliet] How if, when I am laid into the tomb,
  I wake before the time that Romeo
  Come to redeem me? There's a fearful point!
  Shall I not then be stifled in the vault,
  To whose foul mouth no healthsome air breathes in,
  And there lie strangled ere my Romeo comes?
  Romeo, I come! This do I drink to thee.

Juliet drinks and exits.

ACT IV, SCENE 4.
CAPULET'S HOUSE.

Enter Capulet, Lady Capulet and the Nurse.

Lady Cap. Hold, take these keys and fetch more spices.

Nurse. They call for dates and quinces in the pastry°.

Cap. The County will be here with music straight,
  For so he said he would.

Music can be heard.

[Cap] I hear him near. Nurse!
  Go waken Juliet; go and trim her up.
  I'll go chat with Paris. Hie, make haste,
  Make haste! The bridegroom he is come already:
  Make haste, I say.

They all exit.

Pastry: pastry room.

ACT IV, SCENE 5.
JULIET IS LYING IN HER CHAMBER.

Nurse. [Offstage.] Mistress! What mistress! Juliet!
   Fast°, I warrant her, she. *[Nurse enters.]*
   Fie, you slugabed!
   What, not a word? How sound is she asleep!
   I needs must wake her. *[Gently nudges Juliet.]*
   Madam, madam, madam!
   Alas, alas! Help, help! My lady's dead!
   O! Well-a-day that ever I was born.

Enter Lady Capulet.

Lady Cap. What noise is here?

Nurse. O lamentable day!

Lady Cap. What is the matter?

Nurse. Look, look! O heavy day!

Lady Cap. O me, O me! My child, my only life!
   Revive, look up, or I will die with thee!
   Help, help! Call help.

Enter Capulet, Paris, and two servants.

Cap. For shame, bring Juliet forth; her lord is come.

Nurse. She's dead, deceased; she's dead! Alack the day!

Fast: sound asleep.

61

Cap. Ha! Let me see her. Out, alas! She's cold,
  Her blood is settled, and her joints are stiff;
  Life and these lips have long been separated.
  Death lies on her like an untimely° frost
  Upon the sweetest flower of the field.
  All things that we ordained festival
  Turn from their office to black funeral
  Our instruments° to melancholy bells,
  Our wedding cheer° to a sad burial feast;
  Our bridal flowers serve for a buried corpse.

The two servants carry Juliet's lifeless body as they all exit.

Untimely: out of season.   *Instruments:* musical instruments.   *Cheer:* joy.

ACT V, SCENE 1.
STREET IN MANTUA.

Enter Romeo.

Romeo. I dreamt my lady came and found me dead.
  (Strange dream that gives° a dead man leave° to think.)
  And breathed such life with kisses in my lips
  That I revived and was an emperor.

Enter Balthasar.

[Romeo] News from Verona! How now, Balthasar?
  Dost thou not bring me letters from the Friar?
  How doth my lady? Is my father well?
  How doth my Juliet? That I ask again,
  For nothing can be ill if she be well.

Balth. Then she is well°, and nothing can be ill.
  Her body sleeps in Capel's monument°,
  And her immortal part with angels lives
  I saw her laid low in her kindred's vault
  And presently° took post° to tell it you.
  O, pardon me for bringing these ill news.

Romeo. Is it e'en so? Then I defy you, stars!
  Thou knowst my lodging. Get me ink and paper
  and hire post-horses. I will hence tonight.

Gives: allows.   *Leave:* time.   *Well:* in heaven.   *Monument:* tomb   *Presently:*
immediately.   *Took post:* hired post-horses.

65

Balth. I do beseech you, sir, have patience.
   Your looks are pale and wild and do import
   Some misadventure°.

Romeo. No matter. Get thee gone,
   And hire those horses. I'll be with thee straight.

Exit Balthasar.

[Romeo] Well, Juliet, I will lie with thee tonight.
   Let's see for means. O mischief, thou art swift
   To enter in the thoughts of desperate men!
   I do remember an apothecary
   And hereabouts he dwells, which late I noted
   In tattered weeds°, with overwhelming° brows,
   Culling of simples°.
   As I remember, this should be the house.
   Being holiday, the beggar's shop is shut.
   What ho, apothecary!

Apothecary. [Offstage.] Who calls so loud?

Romeo. Come hither, man.

Apothecary enters.

[Romeo]   I see thou art poor.
   Hold, there is forty ducats°.
   Let me have a dram of poison.

Misadventure: bad fortune.   *Weeds:* clothes.   *Overwhelming:* jutting.   *Culling*
of simples: sorting of herbs.   *Ducats:* gold coins.

Apoth. Such mortal drugs I have; but Mantua's law
   is death to any he that utters° them.

Romeo.   Famine is in they cheeks,
   Need and oppression starveth in thine eyes,
   Contempt and beggary hangs upon thy back:
   The world is not thy friend, nor the world's law;
   The world affords no law to make thee rich;
   Then be not poor, but break it° and take this.

Apoth. My poverty and not my will consents.

Apothecary exits and returns with vial.

[Apoth] Put this in any liquid thing you will
   And drink it off, and if you had the strength
   Of twenty men, it would dispatch you straight.

Romeo. There is thy gold—worse poison to men's souls,
   Doing more murder in this loathsome world,
   Than these poor compounds that thou mayst not sell.

Apothecary exits.

Romeo. To Juliet's grave; for there must I use thee.

Utters: sells.   *Break it:* i.e., the law.

ACT V, SCENE 2.
FRIAR LAURENCE IS IN HIS CELL.

Enter Friar John.

Friar. This same should be the voice of Friar John.
  Welcome from Mantua. What says Romeo?
  Or, if his mind be writ, give me his letter.

John. Infectious pestilence° did reign,
  Sealed up the doors°, and would not let us forth,
  So that my speed to Mantua there was stayed°.

Friar. Who bare my letter, then, to Romeo?

John. I could not send it—here it is again.
  Nor get a messenger to bring it thee,
  So fearful were they of infection.

Friar. Unhappy fortune! By my brotherhood,
  The letter was not nice°, but full of charge°,
  Of dear import°, and the neglecting it
  May do much danger.
  Now must I to the monument alone.
  Within these three hours will fair Juliet wake.
  I will write again to Mantua,
  And keep her at my cell till Romeo come.

They both exit.

Pestilence: disease.   *Sealed up the doors:* legal quarantine.   *Stayed:* delayed.
Nice: trivial.   *Charge:* weighty matters.   *Dear import:* great importance.

ACT V, SCENE 3.
THE CAPULET VAULT.

In the tomb, Juliet and Tybalt are laid out and covered by shrouds. Paris stands next to Juliet.

Paris. Sweet flower, with flowers thy bridal bed I strew.

He tosses flowers on her tomb. Whistle is heard offstage.

[Paris] The boy gives warning something doth approach.
  What cursed foot wanders this way tonight
  To cross° my obsequies and true love's rite?

Paris hides as Romeo and Balthasar enter.

Romeo. Hold, take this letter. Early in the morning
  See thou deliver it to my lord and father.
  Give me the light. Upon thy life I charge thee,
  Whatever thou hearest or seest, stand all aloof°
  And do not interrupt me in my course
  Or, by heaven, I will tear thee joint by joint.

Balth. I will be gone, sir, and not trouble you.

Romeo. So shalt thou show me friendship. Take thou that.
  Live, and be prosperous; and farewell, good fellow.

Balthasar exits with Romeo's pouch of coins.

Cross: interfere with.   *Aloof:* at a distance.

Romeo. Thou detestable maw°, thou womb of death,
   Gorged with the dearest morsel of the earth,
   Thus in despite° I'll cram thee with more food.

Paris.   Montague!
   Can vengeance be pursued further than death?
   Condemned villain, I do apprehend thee.
   Obey, and go with me; for thou must die.

Romeo. I must indeed; and therefore came I hither.
   Good gentle youth, tempt not a desperate man.
   Fly hence and leave me. Think upon these gone.
   Put not another sin upon my head
   By urging me to fury. O, be gone!

Paris. I do defy thy conjuration°.
   And apprehend thee for a felon here. *[Draws his rapier.]*

Romeo. Wilt thou provoke me? *[Romeo draws his dagger.]*
   Then have at thee, boy!

They fight and Paris is slain.

[Romeo] O my love! My wife!
   Death, that hath sucked the honey of thy breath,
   Hath had no power yet upon thy beauty.
   Beauty's ensign yet
   Is crimson in thy lips and in thy cheeks,
   And death's pale flag is not advanced there.
   Tybalt, liest thou there in thy bloody sheet?
   Forgive me, cousin!

Maw: stomach.   *In despite:* with malice.   *Conjuration:* entreaty.

[Romeo] Ah, dear Juliet, why art thou yet so fair?
  Here will I remain. Eyes look your last.
  Arms take your last embrace! And lips, O you
  The doors of breath, seal with a righteous kiss
  A dateless° bargain to engrossing° death.
  Come, bitter conduct; come unsavory guide!
  Thou desperate pilot, now at once run on
  The dashing rocks thy seasick weary bark°!
  Here's to my love! *[Drinks the poison.]* O true apothecary!
  Thy drugs are quick. Thus with a kiss I die.

Romeo kisses Juliet and falls next to her bier. Friar enters.

Friar. Romeo! O pale! Who else? What, Paris too?
  And steeped in blood? Ah, what an unkind hour
  Is guilty of this lamentable chance! The lady stirs.

Juliet. O comfortable° Friar! Where is my lord?
  I do remember well where I should be,
  And there I am. Where is my Romeo?

Noise is heard offstage.

Friar. I hear some noise. Lady, come from that nest
  Of death, contagion, and unnatural sleep.
  A greater power than we can contradict
  Hath thwarted our intents. Come, come away.
  Thy husband in thy bosom there lies dead;
  And Paris too. Come, I'll dispose of° thee
  Among a sisterhood of holy nuns.
  Stay not to question, for the watch° is coming.
  Come, go, good Juliet. I dare no longer stay.

Dateless: eternal. *Engrossing:* monopolizing. *Bark:* i.e., Romeo's body.
Comfortable: comforting *Dispose of:* place. Watch: watchman.

Juliet. Go, get thee hence, for I will not away.

Friar exits.

[Juliet] What's here? A cup closed in my true love's hand?
    Poison, I see, hath been his timeless° end.
    O churl°! Drunk all, and left no friendly drop
    To help me after? I will kiss thy lips.
    Haply° some poison yet doth hang on them.

She kisses him and more noise can be heard offstage.

[Juliet] Yea, noise? Then I'll be brief. *[Takes his dagger.]*
    O happy dagger° !
    This° is thy sheath; there rest°, and let me die.

*She stabs herself and falls over Romeo. Enter Capulets,
Montagues, Prince, guards, etc.*

Prince. What misadventure is so early up,
    That calls our person from our morning rest?

Guard. Sovereign, here lies the County Paris, slain;
    And Romeo dead; and Juliet, dead before,
    Warm and new-killed.

Mont. Alas, my liege, my wife is dead tonight!
    Grief of my son's exile hath stopped her breath.
    What further woe conspires against mine age?

Timeless: untimely.   *Churl:* thoughtless man.   *Haply:* hopefully.   *Happy dagger:*
i.e., fortunately there is a dagger nearby.   *This: i.e.,* her breast.   *Rest:* could also
be rust.

Prince. Look, and thou shalt see. Capulet, Montague,
   See what a scourge is laid upon your hate,
   That heaven finds means to kill your joys with love!
   And I, for winking° at your discord too,
   Have lost a brace of kinsmen. All are punished.

Cap. O brother Montague, give me thy hand.
   This° is my daughter's jointure°, for no more
   Can I demand.

Mont.   But I can give thee more;
   For I will raise her statue in pure gold,
   That whiles Verona by that name is known,
   There shall be no figure at such rate° be set
   As that of true and faithful Juliet.

Cap. As rich shall Romeo's by his lady's lie
   Poor sacrifices° of our enmity!

Prince. A glooming° peace this morning with it brings.
   The sun for sorrow will not show his head.
   Go hence, to have more talk of these sad things;
   Some shall be pardoned, and some punished;
   For never was a story of more woe
   Than this of Juliet and her Romeo.

The end.

Winking: shutting my eyes to.   *This: i.e.,* hand of friendship.   *Jointure:* dowry.
Rate: value.   *Poor sacrifices:* pitiful victims.   *Glooming:* cloudy.

Other Fine Titles From
Five Star Publications, Incorporated

Most titles are available through
www.BarnesandNoble.com and www.amazon.com

Shakespeare: To Teach or Not to Teach
By Cass Foster and Lynn G. Johnson
The answer is a resounding "To Teach!" There's nothing dull about this guide for anyone teaching Shakespeare in the classroom, with activities such as crossword puzzles, a scavenger hunt, warm-up games, and costume and scenery suggestions.   ISBN 1-877749-03-6

The Sixty-Minute Shakespeare Series
By Cass Foster
Not enough time to tackle the unabridged versions of the world's most widely read playwright? Pick up a copy of *Romeo and Juliet* (ISBN 1-877749-38-9), *A Midsummer Night's Dream* (ISBN 1-877749-37-0), *Hamlet* (ISBN 1-877749-40-0), *Macbeth* (ISBN 1-877749-41-9), *Much Ado About Nothing* (ISBN 1-877749-42-7), and *Twelfth Night* (ISBN 1-877749-39-7) and discover how much more accessible Shakespeare can be to you and your students.

Shakespeare for Children: The Story of Romeo and Juliet
By Cass Foster
Adults shouldn't keep a classic this good to themselves. This fully illustrated book makes the play easily understandable to young readers, yet it is faithful to the spirit of the original. A *Benjamin Franklin Children's Storybooks Award* nominee. ISBN 0-9619853-3-x

The Adventures of Andi O'Malley
By Celeste Messer

(1) Angel Experiment JR134
Ashley Layne is the richest and most popular girl in school. In an unusual twist, Andi is given the opportunity to know what it's truly like to be Ashley Layne. Travel with Andi as she discovers that things are not always as they seem.   ISBN 0-9702171-0-2

(2) The Broken Wing
Andi is visited by a little angel who needs her help in more ways than one. The angel has broken her wing in a midair collision with another, larger angel and desperately needs Andi to hide her while she heals. Rather than hide her, Andi takes the little angel to school with her where no one could have expected the lessons they would learn! ISBN 0-9702171-1-0

(3) The Gift
Andi receives an assignment from her guardian angel. At first, she's excited, but she becomes furious when she realizes what the job involves. Although Andi tries desperately to get out of completing her assignment, she learns there is no turning back. What happens in the end could only happen to Andi O'Malley! ISBN 0-9702171-3-7

Other Fine Titles From
Five Star Publications, Incorporated

Most titles are available through
www.BarnesandNoble.com and www.amazon.com

(4) Circle of Light

The world is about to be taken over by Zykien, the most evil of all angels of darkness. With the help of the rather odd-looking Miss Bluebonnet, Andi and her friends discover the incredible power of goodness that can result when people work together. Even the Tashonians, the tiniest of creatures, play an important role in restoring peace and love to the world.
ISBN 0-9702171-2-9

(5) Three Miracles

Three young people are in a terrible accident caused by a drunk driver. Their voices are heard—but only by Andi's friend Troy. When he proves to Andi and her sister and brother that he's not making it up, the three voices give them three tasks that will change their lives and the lives of several others forever.
ISBN 0-9702171-4-5

Letters of Love: Stories from the Heart

Edited by Salvatore Caputo
In this warm collection of love letters and stories, a group of everyday people share hopes, dreams, and experiences of love: love won, love lost, and love found again. Most of all, they share their belief that love is a blessing that makes life's challenges worthwhile.   ISBN 1-877749-35-4

Linda F. Radke's Promote Like a Pro: Small Budget, Big Show

By Linda F. Radke
In this step-by-step guide, self-publishers can learn how to use the print and broadcast media, public relations, the Internet, public speaking, and other tools to market books—without breaking the bank! In *Linda F. Radke's Promote Like a Pro: Small Budget, Big Show*, a successful publisher and a group of insiders offer self-publishers valuable information about promoting books.
ISBN 1-877749-36-2

The Economical Guide to Self-Publishing: How to Produce and Market Your Book on a Budget

By Linda F. Radke
This book is a must-have for anyone who is or wants to be a self-publisher. It is a valuable step-by-step guide for producing and promoting your book effectively, even on a limited budget. The book is filled with tips on avoiding common, costly mistakes and provides resources that can save you lots of money—not to mention headaches. A *Writer's Digest Book Club* selection.   ISBN 1-877749-16-8

That Hungarian's in My Kitchen

By Linda F. Radke
You won't want that Hungarian to leave your kitchen after you've tried some of the 125 Hungarian-American Kosher recipes that fill this delightful cookbook. Written for both the novice cook and the sophisticated chef, the cookbook comes complete with "Aunt Ethel's Helpful Hints."   ISBN 1-877749-28-1

Other Fine Titles From
Five Star Publications, Incorporated

Most titles are available through
www.BarnesandNoble.com and www.amazon.com

Kosher Kettle: International Adventures in Jewish Cooking
By Sybil Ruth Kaplan, Foreword by Joan Nathan

With more than 350 recipes from 27 countries, this is one Kosher cookbook you don't want to be without. It includes everything from wheat halva from India to borrekas from Greece. Five Star Publications is donating a portion of all sales of *Kosher Kettle* to MAZON: A Jewish Response to Hunger. A *Jewish Book Club* selection.   ISBN 1-877749-19-2

Passover Cookery
By Joan Kekst

Whether you're a novice or an experienced cook, Passover can result in hours spent hunting down recipes from friends and family or scrambling through piles of cookbooks. Now Passover cooking can become "a piece of cake" with the new book, *Passover Cookery: In the Kitchen with Joan Kekst.* You can create a new, distinctive feast or reproduce the beautiful traditions from your grandmother's Seder with Kekst's easy to follow steps and innovative recipes from her extensive private collection. From daily fare to gourmet, "kosher for Passover" delights have never been easier or more delicious! ISBN 1-877749-44-3

Household Careers: Nannies, Butlers, Maids & More:
The Complete Guide for Finding Household Employment
By Linda F. Radke

Numerous professional positions are available in the child-care and home-help fields. This award-winning book provides all the information you need to find and secure a household job.
ISBN 1-877749-05-2

Nannies, Maids & More: The Complete Guide for Hiring Household Help
By Linda F. Radke

Anyone who has had to hire household help knows what a challenge it can be. This book provides a step-by-step guide to hiring—and keeping—household help, complete with sample ads, interview questions, and employment forms.
ISBN 0-9619853-2-1

Shoah: Journey From the Ashes
By Cantor Leo Fettman and Paul M. Howey

Cantor Leo Fettman survived the horrors of Auschwitz while millions of others, including almost his entire family, did not. He worked in the crematorium, was a victim of Dr. Josef Mengele's experiments, and lived through an attempted hanging by the SS. His remarkable tale of survival and subsequent joy is an inspiration for all. *Shoah* includes a historical prologue that chronicles the 2,000 years of anti-Semitism that led to the Holocaust. Cantor Fettman's message is one of love and hope, yet it contains an important warning for new generations to remember so the evils of the past will not be repeated.   ISBN 0-9679721-0-8

Other Fine Titles From
Five Star Publications, Incorporated

Most titles are available through
www.BarnesandNoble.com and www.amazon.com

The Proper Pig's Guide to Mealtime Manners
By L.A. Kowal and Sally Starbuck Stamp
No one in your family would ever act like a pig at mealtime, but perhaps you know another family with that problem. This whimsical guide, complete with its own ceramic pig, gives valuable advice for children and adults alike on how to make mealtimes more fun and mannerly.
ISBN 1-877749-20-6

Junk Mail Solution
By Jackie Plusch
Jackie Plusch's Junk Mail Solution can help stop the aggravating intrusion of unwanted solicitations by both mail and phone. She offers three easy steps for freeing yourself from junk mailers and telemarketers. The book also includes pre-addressed cards to major mass marketing companies and handy script cards to put by your phones.
ISBN 0-9673136-1-9

Printed in the United States
202503BV00001B/1-105/A